Dark Familiar

ALSO BY ALEDA SHIRLEY

Long Distance (1996)
Chinese Architecture (1986)

Dark Familiar

Aleda Shirley

Sarabande  Books

LOUISVILLE, KENTUCKY

FIRST EDITION

No part of this book may be reproduced without written permission of the publisher. Please direct inquiries to:

Managing Editor
Sarabande Books, Inc.
2234 Dundee Road, Suite 200
Louisville, KY 40205

LIBRARY OF CONGRESS CATALOGING-IN-PUBLICATION DATA

Shirley, Aleda.
    Dark familiar : poems / by Aleda Shirley. — 1st ed.
        p.   cm.
    ISBN 1-932511-35-0 (acid-free paper) — ISBN 1-932511-36-9 (pbk. : acid-free paper).
    I. Title.
    PS3569.H557D37 2006
    811'.54—dc22   2005028004

13-digit ISBN 978-1-932-51135-2 (cloth); ISBN 978-1-932-51136-9 (paper)

Cover image: *Light from Above,* by Charles Carraway. Used by permission of the Mississippi Museum of Art.

Cover and text design by Charles Casey Martin

Manufactured in Canada
This book is printed on acid-free paper.

Sarabande Books is a nonprofit literary organization.

THE KENTUCKY ARTS COUNCIL

The Kentucky Arts Council, a state agency in the Commerce Cabinet, provides operational support funding for Sarabande Books with state tax dollars and federal funding from the National Endowment for the Arts, which believes that a great nation deserves great art.

for my husband
& my parents

Silence is too accurate.

—Mark Rothko

Table of Contents

Dark Familiar

THE STAR'S ETRUSCAN ARGUMENT

I could be almost anywhere, beside the Atlantic
or in the desert, on a boat never designed to sail,
but I'm not, I'm in the hotel of a casino

on an Indian reservation in the deep south,
a sovereign nation in a county still unable
to resolve a murder forty years old. Four a.m.

& my mind's wheeling in huge ambits,
as if through an empty sky, the green numbers
on the digital clock ticking toward morning:

I turn on the television to the hotel channel,
where they teach you how to play roulette & blackjack,
then switch to an old movie I loved in college.

My window opens not to the world but on to the floor
& when I part the curtains the mild gold light
of the lamp is swallowed up by the casino's whiter,

cooler, cleaner light. Half past four & row after row
of people are playing slot machines; driven,
stoic, they don't pull the lever but instead punch

over & over a square lit button that places bets
faster & with less effort, all visceral pleasure,
the smooth glide of expensive equipment, removed.

If the window opened I'd hear the sound of waitresses
pushing drinks, the click of disposable lighters,
the muscular toll of coins hitting metal trays

& beneath all that a fabricated soundtrack of luck & fortune,
money singing, the bruit of machines hitting big.
Their eyes gleam with hope & its opposite,

which is also hope: the tinsel change of a small windfall;
free passes to the buffet, its bounty of crab legs
& fried shrimp, a chef carving thick slabs

of prime rib; or the big score, the million dollars
that would change their lives completely & forever.
These days memory is assembled from consumption's

debris, the promise of happiness or the crumpled containers
in which the promise was wrapped. How quickly
smoke swirling from a hundred cigarettes dissolves

above their heads: invisible systems at work, & God
not looking out for any of us from the inverted
domes in the ceiling that watch & record everything.

Brown, Black on Maroon

When I think about you now, in the middle of the night
when I can't sleep, I'm seized by a frantic
need to pack & yet I can't get my things together,
the things I need & those that can't be replaced if I leave

them behind. I'm wandering through a vast strange
house that bears some resemblance to places
I've actually lived, except the rooms keep opening up
to other rooms, each darker than the one before,

tenebrous corners where I can't imagine placing a chair
or lighting a lamp. There's a view of winter
from a high window, hopeless planes of white
interrupted by a line of trees, the ruins of a tobacco barn

where my grandfather worked half a century ago,
a silver car moving too fast down a country road.
Held, rubbed round like a lucky piece of hematite,
the random facts that lodge in the mind glow

with a promise of revelation: I learned recently
that the statues on Easter Island, which I've seen

in photographs a hundred times, actually face inland;
they do not look out to sea. There was a night,

on an endless drive home from Chicago,
when I saw from the highway a field in flames,
farmers conducting a controlled burn, red swirling
so hard against the sky that the stars moved

backward. All this, all this & more I've left unsaid,
what I feel in the dark room when I'm wildly gathering
up sweaters & photographs & tarnished silver forks,
is why it grows less possible each day to map the void God's

absence has scooped from the world. Death's bearable
when it's your own: you won't be there the next time
the white azaleas ignite on the lawns of the south
& an aria drifts out from the windows of a living room,

or when the sound's coarse, the rattle of news on cable TV,
a dry bitter fall. For a long time I thought of you
as the one who left, but now, in the middle of the night,
the face I see in the window of the speeding car is my own.

BLUE POLES

There's mild comfort in order—alphabetized books,
a well-stocked bar, stacks of folded laundry
scented with lavender. When I was young
I tried to learn the constellations, their shapes
& positions, but it was bewildering, the night sky

milky with city light, the contours too abstract.
As language evolves & acquires words for colors
colors always enter in the same order: black & white,
then red, then green or yellow, & after that the other one,
yellow or green. The fifth color is always a name

for blue. An afterthought, a spectre of green—
yet how blue & nothing else are the hours at three & four a.m.
when a powdery light, sliced up by the blinds,
moves across the bed & a passing car throbs
with hiphop, something stirring & yet not wholly:

you're in the room, in the front seat of the car
& on my arm the trace of your fingers, lozenges
of sun-warmed metal. Out the window
the weight of April darkness, the tidal swirl
of leaves already heavy on the trees: I'm here, I'm here;

you are dead, I insist, your gaze wide as a statue's,
the moon laying plates of zinc on the dark street.
Blue the shadows wrapping your face, the gauges & dials
on the dashboard, the cat at the end of the bed,
invisible but for two sharp points of phosphorous.

Flow blue soup bowls in the dining room,
dried hydrangea, clematis climbing the window:
it isn't much but it's all I have in this
hypnagogic state that persists through dawn
& high hot noon & midday errands—the grocery store,

the post office, the farmer's market—& then on into dusk,
a lush canal pouring on to the terrace, the glasses
of clear cold gin, past the city truck spraying
for mosquitoes, swirls of twilight augmenting twilight,
& then night again, the uneasy climb toward sleep.

Phantom Pain

And now only faith could make me certain
that beneath the mulch in the garden the bulbs of the daffodils
& the bulbs of the tulips double themselves
as they sleep through winter. In front of the mirror
a blown black vase that held strands of forsythia last April.
The dead leave us incomplete. It didn't occur
to me the emptiness would be permanent,
that nothing that came after would ease the ache
as the cold rains of October blew out the pilot lights,
& what I was once attached to, what was once attached to me,
would glint in the welkin & go truant.
I count the cats at their Hadley bowls in the morning,
as I would count the leaves of the redbud,
the old selves lingering, like smoke or cedar,
in coats in the hall closet, camel's hair & tweed,
waxed cotton. Once I glimpsed my face drifting
through the transom, past a bough of cold stars.
At some point the dead outnumber the living,
except in the silly brocatel of the physical world
where I hear in the sibilance of gingko leaves falling,
one night a year, their footsteps as they walk,
with no thought of me, through corridors
of the underworld. I imagine them together,

a wing of the beloved, but my dead

have their own dead to find & so must disperse,

unable to remain in an assembly of my devising.

I wonder if they gather, seasonally, in a vast hall,

the air filtered into fake euphoria, like a casino's,

a serried music of wealth urging them to wager more,

& on the great window a pale outline of bones.

Perhaps when I join them it will be different.

For now they have their own resolve & muted ardor—

skin & moon at room temperature,

hothouse phlox, blooming in the lunar seas.

BLUE OVER ORANGE

October's first cold day & when I get in the car
my breath forms a brief chrysanthemum
on the inside of the windshield & I'm aware,

suddenly, of all the yellow leaking from the world,
the lost green veins of the leaves. On my list
of errands the last stop is the video store where

the movies I watched in college are now classified
as *Cult Favorites* or *Classics* & the beautiful boy
who works the counter rolls his eyes when I take out

the Truffaut for the dozenth time. *Not again,* he says.
He's nice to everyone, but he sees me, if he sees me at all,
as an adult woman in a dark coat, with an expensive bag.

We touch only when we exchange money. The lobby
of a narrow French apartment, an allée of poplars:
those are scenes from a movie, not my life. I'm unlikely

to rent the movies that excite him: Japanese animation,
a documentary on mountain climbing, seventies concert films
from before he was born. Hours later, at home

with my glass of bourbon, he's with me still, & I think,
out of nowhere I tell myself, about how when I was thirteen
& we lived overseas I saw middle-aged NCOs

with beer guts & sunburned scalps walking the streets
of San Angeles City, holding the hands of girls
not much older than I was, girls paid to be adoring,

who covered their mouths when they giggled
& wore strange yellow nylons the color of no human skin.
When we'd walk down those streets, my friends & I,

our raffia bags stuffed with devalued pesos,
Filipino boys would sit on their haunches & make
wet clucking noises at us. Back then I imagined the misery

of the teenaged prostitutes, though not in any detail,
& the men's daughters stateside, reading
Tiger Beat in their rooms, trying on Yardley lipstick.

Later I thought about the wives, left behind
at Lackland or Minot or Clovis, the scent
of coffee, Salems, Emeraude, & something that may

or may not have been history pushing them to the sides
of their own lives; now I think of the men—
how little of life turns out to be a choice, after all,

& the way those choices we do make
can transform beauty into pathos or desire
into commerce. We are, all of us, almost alike.

April Fifteenth

Taxes due, the anniversary of Henry James's death,
& a brilliant sky rinsed of pollen & glare by yesterday's
record rain. From the magnolia in my front yard

the Mexican workers who are here to fix
the foundation of my house have hung their lunches
in grocery bags—they look like large dull light bulbs

that have burned out. When the foreman leaves
on an errand I see the youngest worker struggling to pull
a water hose to the back. Through the window

I tell him there's another hose in the garage that will reach,
but he doesn't understand a word I'm saying. Finally
I point & say *aqua* & all six of them brighten

with comprehension, although I realize later I used
the Latin word, not the Spanish one. The house
was slowly sinking, stairstep cracks along the brick,

fractures in the plaster, the floor of the back bedroom
sloping three inches; one night, we heard a huge crash:
the window frame so distorted the glass shattered

in jagged shards, transparent puzzle pieces
on the fruitwood table. Later, after the holes
have been dug, the forsythia & sweet olive bent

out of the way, the lunches eaten, they jack the house up
& it shudders & pops, the cats head for somewhere
dark & safe, & before I figure out what's going on

I wonder if the workers are playing soccer
on the roof or if there's an earthquake. By dusk
they're mixing mortar, repointing brick, & in the yard

a grackle, a bluejay, & two cardinals peck
at the damp grass. I'd love to draw some lesson
from this, that things we can't see hold us up

& it's possible for those things to be repaired.
But I don't buy it; I think how you are
is how you are, that the level of joy or meaning

on the most ordinary Wednesday afternoon
is the level of joy or meaning you're stuck with.
Years from now I'll think of the lunches hanging

from the tree & how at the end of a long day
I heard music in the foreign recognizable sounds
of the workers calling to my neighbor's dog.

THE MINOR OF WHAT WE FELT

Yesterday, in a friend's garden, I listened to the distant
hum of traffic on the interstate as the sun, seeking
bright planes, stuttered through the oaks & across

the cyan mirror of the water. What I can't count as easily:
needles on the pine tree, individual slashes
of warm fragrant rain, loss. My friend is in Spain,

with her children. I didn't hear the phone ring but suddenly!
her voice, as the answering machine picked up,
& then a stranger's, asking her to call back ASAP.

My mind moved from the weather of the past
into the past, a cistern of sound & wind.
Under the zinc-white sky, a winter so bitter

the world was wiped clean by cold silver gloves.
That was the year we drank coffee in a motel lobby
& said goodbye. My scarf fell to the floor,

cabala of canary & cerise. One more drink…
the off-chance that another conversation would reassemble
the broken tiles into a smooth expanse of marble

or ice. But the bar was closed, dusty bottles of bourbon
& gin locked behind a grate. *I must be going,* you said.
A geode, a silk umbrella with a broken spoke—I have kept

these things as I would have kept the pieces of sunset
shattering on the water, the ingot on my arm,
my friend's bright *hello, leave a message at the tone,*

but I've lost my taste for the indistinct, the luminously
suggestive. I want heft, the long strands ordered
& restrained by narrow ribbons of metal grosgrain. Mystery

is too easily destroyed. And it takes so little:
the ordinary baize light of morning,
an hour at the library, or simply knowing who to ask.

Plaint

Here, the sky to the north is a bright slate blue,
full of portent & ready to let go.
But it won't snow, the leaves have just peaked.
And the gingkos, the one by the library on State Street
& the one two houses down on Pinehurst—

those leaves know the past is bright & warm
& can be held, briefly, aloft. But a night,
if not this one, then Thursday or Friday, will change
all this & the trees will spend their wealth
recklessly into the street & onto the lawns:

I'll hear it as I try to sleep, the sound of falling
beneath other sounds. And the next day
someone will pay someone else
to rake them, blow them, bag them;
up & down the street black vinyl bags

that might be mistaken, from the distance of the sky,
for treasure washed up, bags of gold
swathed in seaweed. On the weather channel
scraps of azure mean snow is general in Kentucky.
For years I waited for dust to settle on the past

& dim the auric-rose of maple leaves
on a path in Cave Hill, to soften the tatted sleet
on the windshield of my old blue car, but this dust
is like that of a volcano, a lie, a lens distorting dawn
& sunset into lustre, for years after the event.

SONG OF THE ABDUCTED

The trees are full of owls. At night thousands
of them stare at me through the sunroom windows.
The phone rings; it is my dead friend, calling
from Boston. She talks & talks,
but I can get nothing out, I am choking

on questions. The owls' heads move so quickly
they do not seem to move. It started
when I was a child: late one night my father
stopped the car at a roadside park & dozed,
a silver thermos of coffee in his lap. I slept too,

in the back, & woke to a deer looking
in the window, its nose pressed against the glass,
eyes huge & glossy. The next thing I knew
it was morning & we were driving over the bridge
into Memphis. Later from a hotel room

I saw helicopters a few feet from the window,
but there was no noise. At night
everyone comes back to me eventually,
this one I loved & that one.
The air grows sharp as copper & there's

a beautiful green light that deepens
like water; I move through it slowly
but it is not wet & I never surface, no matter
how hard I kick my legs. Inside myself
I am several hours behind myself. From one summer

I recall flowers: sunflowers peering like faces
over a fence, knotted peonies fallen on the lawn.
For months, after I fell in love, I couldn't sleep
until dawn: nothing wedged itself between me
& the darkness. But passion dimmed to an ashy

smudge on the mirror & through the fanlight
I saw a collar of dead stars. The rumors you've heard
are true: behind danger lurks danger. Down
the street a house is on fire. Red light courses
through the room & I feel smoke like sticky oil

on my arms, the warm spot where the cat
was sleeping. When I come to I am peering
into the blue face of the television.
There is snow & in the snow a hint of static,
something cold & shifty I cannot turn off.

The Customary Mysteries

When they transferred the site of Hades to the air
the Stoics brought the dead into closer proximity
with the living & so for a time the sky

was full of souls. Away from home I often wake
disoriented & febrile, but in the past year
when I've stayed somewhere high above the ground—

a hotel overlooking the gulf, a borrowed apartment
thirty storeys over Chicago where at sunset
snow fell, flakes of flame in an inland sea—

I woke with the sense of being in my own bed.
We're subjects of two worlds: the daylit one,
solid & consecutive, where we meet our friends,

our families, the charming stranger in line
at the post office, & the one at night where
the border between past & present blurs

& we've the chance of a connection, however fugitive,
with people who are faraway, the dead,
the gods. For the ancient Greeks the psyche

had no function except in its leaving of the body,
though sometimes it would blaze briefly
in the trance of fainting or when facing death.

From the hotel I watched a section of newspaper
blown from someone's balcony swoop & dip
& glide for several minutes above the beach,

the thermals made visible in a way they aren't
by birds, who can move themselves, or a kite,
for which I first mistook it, guided by a human hand.

I wanted to think of it as a soul ascending,
perhaps that of my friend who died suddenly at forty,
some refractory & lissome residue of who he was

lingering on, but the sky was littered with planes
pulling banners advertising happy hours & water parks,
with satellites & space debris & ovals of ozone:

there's no longer enough room. And the world,
fulgent & resolute, clicks on, its vision the same
as a casino's: to keep the wheels turning.

Wisdom

Before me, in an oval of lamplight, a list, the names
of the first thirty-nine men from Metcalfe County, Kentucky,
inducted into the army in 1917 & sent on to train
at Camp Taylor: among them, Elzie B. Pedigo
of Good Luck, Jesse Gibbons of Cyclone, Henry Brints
of Wisdom, & from Summer Shade Mike Steel Jennings,

Ches Herriford, Melvin Vance, James Herriford,
& Waller Franklin Shirley. Imagine them
moving down the road under rustling sweetgums,
the fields on either side of them sloping
into sinkholes, a pale-yellow band of sky to the east.
Half a century later one of them would show me

his gas mask, hanging from a beam in the smokehouse,
his uniform, his Silver Star for valor & challenge me
to pick him out in the wide-angle photograph of his unit,
& I did, finding him by looking for the shape
of my face & that of my father. He'd stretch out
in stiff coveralls by the woodstove after morning chores

& in warm weather rinse his hair in rainwater collected
in a barrel—hair so white & thick it looked veined.

He could remember his father talking about
the Civil War, his father's father talking about the year
without a summer. I don't know how many
of the other thirty-eight remained in the Meuse/Argonne,

Chateau-Thierry, Belleau Wood—my grandfather
came home, to a small farm & the girl he married
on Christmas Day of 1920. And so on with life,
a stillborn baby, then three daughters & a son,
& a thousand thousand changes: electricity & plumbing
& cars, a second war & another & then an invisible one

that didn't end in his lifetime; I remember watching,
on a black & white TV in my grandfather's farmhouse,
an American astronaut walk through space,
the planet shining behind him. Every life has
such vaults, when time sprains it in half or thirds.
When he died, in 1973, the county's old veterans

insisted they could carry his coffin & they did,
their frail battered hands tucked under the flag,
& glittering across the churchyard at Wisdom
a grounded white, formerly the air.
In Paris another useless declaration of peace.
We like to imagine the future as something

we soar toward, but it may be more like falling,
until finally, under the weight of fathoms of darkness,
edges dissolve & colors disappear. Eventually
even ghosts grow so narrow & transparent that,
with a last dutiful flicker, they vanish entirely
into the nearest green, or the dark.

CONVERGENCE: NUMBER 10, 1952

I know it was spring, the tulips late, blooming
after Derby, & so long ago that during
those months a steady beat throbbed constantly
in the background, Andy Gibb, Andrea True,

Donna Summer, & rain rasping on the window unit
in your bedroom, the old trees lining Third Street,
the low hectic voices of people who drank too much,
one of us young, the other middle-aged,

despondent. You told me you loved the rain,
the feel of it on your skin; I remember your saying
this many, many times, as we sat in a bar
or in your kitchen, drinking bourbon, drinking beer,

but only once did we walk, pointlessly, in the rain,
past an old stone fence down the block
to the Catholic church. One night, from a car
stopped at Third & Bloom, Jefferson Starship blasted:

the windows open & pollen on the surfaces
of your walnut furniture, the sleigh bed

where I lay in your arms. *If only you believed...*
then the light changed & I could hear a girl's voice

from the phone booth on the corner. At first
only her tone pierced the rain, then words:
she was begging someone to see her,
to let her come over, wailing I *love you, I love you*

& opening the door of the phone booth a little
so the light would go out & she could disappear
into darkness. I recognized her:
she'd lived in my dorm the year before.

The phone started ringing, though I hadn't seen
her hang up, & each ring seemed as though it
would be the last but wasn't. I could sense
her crying even after she stopped crying; it stayed

in the air a long time. I felt sorry for her.
I want to feel luckier than she was, safe
& warm & loved, but I didn't, not really;
for the first time I understood desperation

is not always due to circumstance. Rain outside,
rain in the mirror & then the rain
went out of the mirror, but I could see
the wet darkness in the folds of the sheets

where you slept. Stirring for a moment you turned
toward the wall. I moved from the window
then back: a pair of headlights dividing air
too silver for a seam, the girl already gone.

TEMPO RUBATO

This afternoon between rows of tulips blooming
along the wide walk to my front door—red tulips
hiding black stars inside, black stars outlined in gold—

my old apricot cat, who turns twenty next week,
sniffed the chinaberry bushes & rubbed her shoulders
across the warm aggregate. The plangent sound

from her throat drifted up through the magnolias
& seemed to hang there. A cloud crossed the sun,
withdrawing for a moment the day's brilliance

though not the glare, everything briefly suspended
in an envelope of silence & green. I once read
that the shortsighted see red more distinctly

than those who discern distant things clearly,
the elongated eye altering not only detail but color.
Last week at a dinner party someone suggested

my bathroom needed updating, the pale-pink tiles
& fifties fixtures, although when I stand in there
I hear, not the sea exactly, but the ocean I perceived

inside a conch shell held to my ear as a child in Kentucky.
At sunset the western window steeps the room in gold,
like the corner of an old church. Through the window

I hear sprinklers in the side yard, programmed
for the wrong time, the world outside wet & hissing
under a perfectly clear sky. Across the face of the moon

a plane passes, a C-130 from the reserve base
& what's left of the moon scatters broken ladders
& empty doors across the yard. The motion detector

on the terrace blazes on, but it's only a raccoon,
panicked & blinded, escaping through the pierced
brick wall of the garage. Numbers are the easiest way

to calculate distance—though when distances grow
too vast we measure things in light—but I've little use
for them anymore, their soigné roister, their denotative limits.

What purpose to count the years that remain:
I never thought I would be spared. But how do I
account for the wild spinning of my inner compass

as various darks, inside & out, swirl around time's
official change: a single second ticking by, all the clocks
in this house suddenly wrong, another hour lost.

THE DEEP

I always forget how ugly so much of Florida is,
the endless parts where you don't have a view
of the sea or even a sense of water nearby, hidden & mute.
And then suddenly a bridge, huge strides of steel,
& it all comes back, why I'm here, why everyone is here,

the cars & SUVs & pickups clogging Highway 98.
I grew up in a town much like this, full of families,
stiff with sunburn, lined up at crab shacks
or to play wacky golf, turning in at the outlet mall;
sullen teenagers laughing too loudly in the elevators,

uneasy in their new bodies; the lurid colors
of drinks & beach balls & visors. In South Carolina,
thirty years ago, my father tried to teach me to drive
on abandoned air force roads deep in a pine forest,
but I never got the hang of the manual transmission

so my impressions from that time are those
of a passenger, a spectator, as if my life were a series
of TV shows I watched from a backseat window,
a travelogue of the same beach town over and over.
Today from the fifteenth floor of a seaside hotel

I heard the sound of children swimming, milder
& more musical than the jazz on the radio,
& from the bed all I could see was sky & gulf—
not two blues, but a dozen, some of them deepening to green,
another losing itself to gray. For light I've arranged

three options: dark, the blackout curtains closed;
dazzling & lacustrine, the doors a transparent rectangle;
or dim, the lamps draped with scarves
& soft bandannas in shades of rose & pale-red—
three sealed & uncommunicating vessels of afternoon.

High above the world, I feel like I'm practicing
leaving the world, falling into beauty emptied
of everything but variations on a single color.
Then the front desk calls: a tropical storm's on the way
& I turn on the TV & see its red spoked symbol

gamboling across the gulf. Landfall's tomorrow night
so my plan is to leave early, outrun the weather.
Already the hotel staff is gathering up umbrellas,
taking down cabanas, wheeling stacks
of pale peach towels inside. A few miles north,

at Eglin, airmen are evacuating planes inland
& I remember, from a lifetime ago, my father & I

watching F4s leave the Grand Strand
when a hurricane threatened that coast,
great silver birds on a flyway to the end of the world.

FIN DE SIÈCLE

The remote by the sofa, the cell in my bag—I check them both:
no missed calls. Twenty years ago, my phone was red,

the one you called me on, the first time, & then many times
after that, from a hotel room in New York & I saw in my mind

the city—whole lives going on behind rows of lighted windows—
while I sat on the bed in my studio apartment,

the one clean white room I'd wanted after our bad year.
Fly to me, I wanted to say, but we didn't speak in such ways,

we kept always some distance & the distance between
Manhattan & Louisville was not enough. I left that apartment

& you hated the dark blue walls of my new rooms;
you said you hated them, but it was something else,

a rift, & all summer I sat at night in a wicker chair,
listening to Sylvia Sims. Back then one rented phones

& I wonder where mine is now, in what lost layer
of a Kentucky landfill. It will not decay in my lifetime.

It did not decay in yours. There are no phones in the other world
& after I dream of you I can spend all day planning

how to respond the next time we speak. How do I measure
distance now? Wreathed in orange & silver leaves

the white-faced cat curls up in the lawn chair.
The Japanese maple appears to die in the throes of great flame,

incarnadine & fever, but the water table will shift
in three or four months, the days lengthen,

the leaves return. A mockingbird, imitating a cardinal,
rouses the cat. I rejoice. Then I remember.

THREE BLACKS IN DARK BLUE

A thousand years ago, the early eighties, New Year's Eve,
& we're driving to your apartment
for champagne & smoked fish at midnight,
the sky lit with clouds, chalk-white,
the car buoyant with warmth, a gondola, a sleigh.

On the way we passed my psychiatrist's house, narrow,
three-storeyed, & when I saw his lighted windows,
the Manx like a cameo in one,
a chatoyant shadow in another, I ached with longing
& considered how, on Tuesday & Friday afternoons,

someone driving by the midcentury medical building
downtown might have seen, if it were raining
or gray & cold, a lamplit window on the seventh floor,
ours for an hour. By then I'd read enough
Freud to know I'd have been in love with my doctor

had he been old & ugly or short with bad skin,
but he wasn't old & he wasn't ugly,
& even now when I close my eyes I can sometimes see

the cotton shirts he favored, plaids so fine
they looked like solid fields of indigo or pale-orange.

Happy new year, million dollars, you said,
even though two hours remained of the old one
& I was reluctant to let it go. Your eyes,
keylit like a movie star's, flickered from the street
to the rearview mirror. Something's always

being mistaken for something else, & I haven't
even mentioned my father, who has outlived you.
I've since learned how artfully you dispersed your feelings,
even as I shimmered with my own betrayal,
beside you on the front seat, & how calculated

was my value to you: a few blocks east,
another woman, the one you married, pined for you,
making the best of a night emptied of fizz & ferment.
When I left the next morning frost
had claimed every transparent object, except the window

where you stood drinking tea. A crunch of footsteps:
but it was the mailman walking across stiff silver grass.
Something uneasy in the motion of your hands
made me think, as I hacked away at ice
on the windshield, of birds. Why did you stand there.

Why did you just stand there & I love a man
I had largely invented. And how is it possible,
from a silence I've never disturbed or escaped,
to locate the precise moment everything ended,
even though it went on & on, forever.

Moving Violation

An itch, an irritant, a flight of nervous birds
disrupting twilight. For months guilt manifests
itself in small ways & I hardly notice; I pour a glass
of wine, I answer the phone & when it's cold & sunny

the car smells of leather & smoke. Sated, I'm outside
reading a book on the theory of color & the day's
bright, sunlight on the glass-topped table spangled
like the foil pinwheels displayed outside

the seaside shops I remember from childhood.
The sun's constant, but then, without warning,
satisfaction shifts into something more.
Betrayal is a game, in which the score is tied.

There should be another way to move forward
through time, a convertible two-seater & no posted
limit. Whether or not ardor is really chemical,
its effect is, traces in the brain slinking into wrist

& thigh. And how ultimately useless the palliatives
of chocolate, layered in dull gold boxes,

& too much sleep, or cheating & its counterfeit heights.
I burned the letter, as if evidence were incarnation

of trespass. That was the least of it, occupying
nothing compared to the space thought occupies after.
Lunch at the museum café, a quarter hour spent
choosing postcards in the gift shop. Then on the way

back a speeding ticket I struggled to explain away.
So many strategies to restore the ordinary:
I say something simple about the sun backlighting
a tangle of vines & brush at the bottom of the garden,

or breaking news: a high speed car chase
on the west coast, a four alarm fire in a Boston warehouse,
weather in another hemisphere. Local weather,
a chance of rain & the day running out finally,

the garden trammeled with panes of twilight.
The sum of these things is large; from them
life is construed. Not from moments of redemption.
And a secret is nothing more than something no one tells.

Purple, White and Red

In the wake of your death, twisting silver koi
& something that looks like the pale pebbled glass
from a smashed windshield. The figure of the Virgin
as she appeared in the window of an office building

in Florida, among the theme parks & golf courses
& souvenir shops. *A miracle; petroleum*
in the treated glass reacting to salt air;
mass delusion—there are more than three worlds

though two are enough, this one & the other.
In the wake of your death, champagne;
an oscillating fan, its blades loosely caged;
& distraction: an avenue of shops flickering

with enameled bangles & stacks of orange boxes.
If the dead could ask questions, imagine the racket
that would fill the huge silences wheeling
through everything: yes, yes, I remember that night,

the motel shining its lights toward us
through propellers of rain; Japanese lanterns

strung in the airport bar; the myth of black tulips.
For months I hardly spoke a word;

I read mysteries in the bright glass box
of my study until afternoon heat sent me
to the shuttered bedroom with its ceiling fan
& carafe of ice. No point in filling a vase

with crepe myrtle—it shattered across the dressing table
at the slightest stir: the fan, a cat jumping
to the window, the moon arriving in daylight,
a ghost of its future self. *What's wrong.*

Those I loved asked & asked until finally
something else terrible happened & I could answer
with that. In the wake, silence, like a mirror
where the silver's gone completely opaque.

THE YELLOW POINT

The floor's terrazzo, the store a deliberate maze;
after a while your eye seizes on sunlight
through distant doors, silver & unreal. First,
the sweaters, stacks of them, butter-yellow

& green & violet. I want them all, I want the scarves
twisted around fake trees & the lipsticks lined up
in shining cases, the pale turquoise sheets
with their million thread counts,

the delicate glasses shaped for this year's drink.
At home violet fills the middle third of the mirror.
On the bed are jackets, arms askew,
that go well with violet or don't—I no longer care.

Soap shaped like shells, sandalwood & freesia,
tea bagged in delicate silk. The kettle shrills.
I want the sweater I put on hold & the one
I didn't find, black with long tight sleeves.

The one I wear drips with tags in three places. Outside
light rain, then sleet, clicking through the live oak.

I want to go home is not what I'm thinking
but it is something like that. On television

there's a commercial about someone who managed—
a taxi in the snow, bells the perfect distance ringing,
faces in the doorway. Then a voiceover, the soft sell.
Some is imprecise: eventually you're required to stop.

It is easier to want nothing. Easier to want everything
& keep going. If the doorbell rings it will be a delivery:
more to open. Knife through tape & on the bed
soft wads of tissue paper I make smaller with my fists.

Forever Is Deciduous

In the attic of my parents' house two suitcases,
brown Samsonite from the fifties, filled with letters
they wrote during my father's tours of duty:
airmail envelopes, bordered in bright blue & red,
& immediately apparent the ones from Viet Nam
because in the corner where the stamp should be

is the word *Free* in my father's hand. But this isn't
about their devotion to one another, or other details
that interest me now: my mother's turquoise Olivetti
whose font mimicked cursive writing, the place names
that since then have changed & sometimes changed again:
Formosa, Red China, Saigon. In the sixties mail

came twice a day, at least to the small post office
in the Kentucky town where my mother & I waited.
When I was seventeen I was surrounded in college
by people protesting the war my father was fighting;
in the dorm, pay phones in the hall & on the nightly news,
a presidency shattering in slow motion.

Recently I learned that my grandfather, who enlisted
in the Army in 1917, ran into his brother Blakey

in a battlefield mess hall in France, having had no idea
he had even joined up. I don't know where this happened
or what they said or how they felt—everyone
who might have known these things is dead.

I've spent much of the past week configuring
a new computer, installing software, transferring
documents & photographs. When my old computer
crashed I immediately ordered its replacement,
overnight shipping, *I don't care how much it costs.*
What did I do before email? If my grandfather's letters

survive I've never seen them, even though I have
his uniform & a wide angle photograph of the ship
that returned him to America, thousands of soldiers
on the decks as it docked in Newport News. *Be here now*
was a slogan lobbed about during my childhood,
a bumper sticker on VW vans; back then it sounded

cool to me & I wrote it out in bubble letters
on the cover of my loose-leaf notebook. Then
for a long time it evoked the sillier elements of that era,
tie-dyed shirts & druggy music & people whose adulthoods
proved problematic, given what they'd stood for
as kids; how is it for the better part of my life
I failed to see its sibylline quality, the simplest truth.

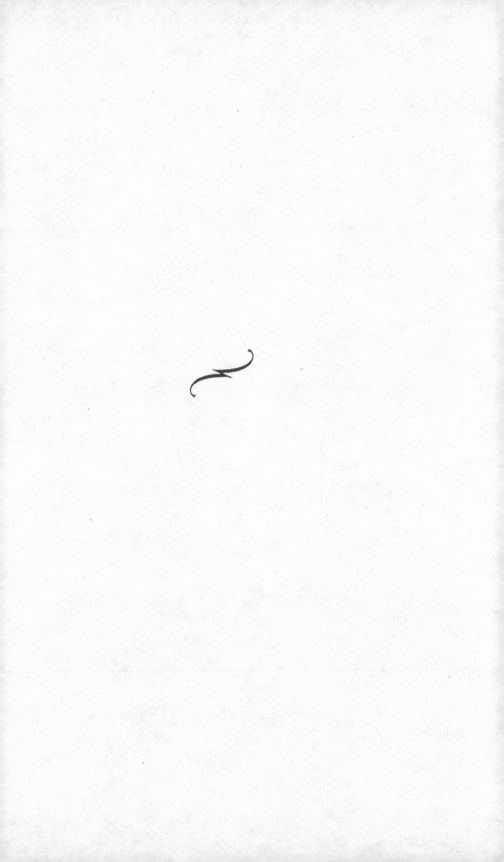

The Asphodel Fields

In its liquid form water's incompressible
& yet a river moves not only through space
but through time. When I lived by the river

it rose ten feet in a single night—there
were petals on the surface, carnelian flecks
from a Judas tree. A boy waved from a ledge

of blue light, but it must have been the bridge,
or a barge lifted to eye-level by the flood.
Where is he now. And you, where are you.

From my pale living room, I imagine a chamber,
cool & hushed, with something not quite
informative droning on in the background, news

or a documentary about a disaster twenty years ago.
Rare minerals, veins of silver looping
through the walls, gems piled high in the corner—

all yours now, but it's useless wealth,
not negotiable in the underworld. Through
my window, noctilucent clouds & more green,

darker now, all of it waste, the one color plants
don't use, the color they shed. So much for hope,
the promise of rebirth. How you must hate

that penumbral room, the shades who drift by
in pairs or small groups, twittering like bats.
I wonder, not for the first time, if you can hear me

or if, like a dark god, you know little of what
goes on in the upper air, except banes & oaths
invoking you. I tried to tell you about

the mirrored willows merging with the real ones,
a myopic fusion of light & brown water,
& of the man on the far shore rowing

a spectral boat through the doorway of his house.
But no one warned me about the countless
tributaries of the Styx that skein through a life.

Snagged in the dark poplars, a scrap of cloth,
a grocery bag, the last material evidence
of a soul. I've waited long enough: it's time I began

paring down to what's indispensable for evening
& leave the wild arithmetic of regret to vanish
in the depths of water's chromal motion.

Four Darks in Red

Along the top of the canvas a band of anthracene
that is God or the absence of God
or someone's ingenuous belief in Him.
Then a slight shimmer of red. In the painting's

upper half an inky rectangle with fading edges,
a correlative for the cold sky over Chicago,
the upper reaches of clouds that obscure & brighten
& obscure again the windows, & finally

the atmosphere in which brilliant air thins to music.
That none of these things is dark or inky or red
doesn't mean you can't recognize them:
their interior wilderness is intact, their boreal mien.

There came a point, he said, *when it was impossible
to paint the human figure without mutilating it.*
And so we're left to fix feeling in objects:
the lines of cars on Chestnut Street, last night's glass

of white burgundy, the morning sky carnelian
over shadow. In the lower margin, umber & bronze-red,

the surface librating even in reproductions.
And it is light: the lobby's travertine floor,

the caramel leather on the Mies chairs,
the vast surface of the lake where jagged pieces of ice
pitch & narrative disappears in incalescence,
sheer oil & effort. If I weren't so tired, I could see

all this from the window of the high-rise apartment
& land for a moment in someone else's life,
perhaps the woman with the papillon waving for a cab,
all the oblongs fraying into cadmium, then prayer.

Spliced Solo

One usable track from four all-night sessions
& the solo in that cobbled together from bits & pieces.
But when you hear it the beauty's unbroken;
you don't perceive juncture. For a long time
I didn't understand the point in denying it,

insisting that the fucked-up valedictories of our lives,
the chromatic fiascos of the heart careening on
like weather, for years, are somehow consecutive,
but he did, & vehemently, right up to the *noir* rebus
of his death. For a long time I didn't understand sin,

its bells of arsenic & snow, though I recognized a jones
for moving on, the seasonal orison to flight
as rhododendron leaves rattle their shredded gold,
or all that he squandered, wadding up his looks,
black & white glamour shots left behind

in fleabag hotels for some stranger to toss out
or keep & sell, a lifetime later, on the internet.
As violet's full spectrum appears at dusk,
I hear in the retroactive blunted affect
of his phrasing a voice whispering *I mean you,*

but he doesn't, he's chainsmoking & talking
long distance to an old flame. Caught in the tine of a tree,
the moon—& in that lunar clamor, a horn or a vocal,
keen enough to metabolize the protein of an angel,
but ending, instead & by mistake, in a minor key.

In the Cathedral

High in the trees the wisteria is blooming, early this year,
as the camellias have been late. And the wrens have returned,
the brace of cardinals who nested in the camellias

last spring. By now everything I'm ever going to tell you
is determined, a sum that can only diminish.
A cold front's blowing in, through sumac & pine,

though there was no snow as I gathered
bills & catalogues & magazines,
the dogwood a single flambeau

with a thousand tongues burning against an argent sky.
Instead a steady click of sleet, hyaline,
disappearing as it touched grass & leaf & wrist,

the stiff white rag of an envelope.
Even before I opened it I knew you were dead.
Who, in the postmodern world, discovers news this way,

when all around us the matte black mouths
of sleek equipment offer to deliver information
instantly? Perhaps only those of us who live a share

of our lives in a trance—the hidden portion,
sheer & candent, floating up into a frozen sky.
And mine, just one of a seraglio of voices, keening,

stone tiles cold beneath my feet, the choir empty,
I'll not wear out the garden with the grief
I bring to it daily: the trees, the weave of sorrel & smalt

in which I spot a pair of eggs, the miniature gardenias
bruised where they're touched. I've audited the books
& discovered I've consumed more than I've preserved,

all those hours carelessly tossed, loose dark change,
in the bottom of a bag. Bequeathed nothing by you,
I must again begin saving or live less dearly.

Contes

The rooms of childhood, the pale-blue one
with a yellow wicker desk & shutters protecting
its frail transparent coolness from the west Texas sun,
the room at the beach house in Virginia, rows of shells
lined up on the windowsill, their pale powdery surfaces.

Yellow tulips in Mrs. Sherrin's garden, the day
Fabienne gathered dozens of them in the skirt
of her smocked dress & ran to me. Later we sat
by the pond turning the pages of *The Lonely Doll,*
as goldfish schooled & dispersed & gathered themselves

back up again. A walk to the museum on a May morning,
Jere in a white linen jacket, so radiant in the sunlight
it deflected, for a little while, his wild capacity
for suffering. Shadows on the bottom of the pool
where I spent much of that summer, its polished blue sides.

The fragrance of my grandfather's barn,
hay & horses & old leather; the orchard where I went
with my father & Linda & her father & brothers
& how strong they seemed, our fathers,
when they opened pecans by cracking them

against other pecans in their fists. And snow,
the snow at our house on Front Street & how
it dissolved in the river until the river froze solid,
Mike making sure the Volvo would start.
Thinking of those things, trying to recover them,

is like moving an incandescent object toward something wet:
they never touch because between them always
is a zone of evaporation. But it's not that simple,
not really; sometimes there's a yellowing,
as in an old photograph, & for a moment

I mistake it for brilliance, some lost moment bright
& flaring, but then the reds fade, everything
turns a featureless uniform blue, & I realize again
that the past is water, fluid, & were it not for the vessel
containing it, entirely without dimension.

THE DISINTEGRATION OF AFTERNOON

Western light slants across the dining room,
the porch drowned in shadow, the oaks & dogwoods
losing their green to imagined violet. And there,
beneath the magnolia with darker glossier leaves

than its fraternal twin on the opposite side
of the drive, I see two figures, clearly,
although as the light deepens their limbs grow
vague, as if they or the cloth they wear were woven

of smoke. What I can't see, what I don't know,
is if this is a moment of greeting or farewell.
There are many reasons people embrace,
but I can think of only one why a man would pull

a woman toward him by the strand of pearls
she wears. Sometimes I can hardly remember you,
only the loss of you, as today when the lengthening light
imposes odd divisions on the lawn, pruning

the mimosa & monkey grass, the wisteria.
How many options? Heaven, hell, nothing;

paradise, reincarnation, nothing. For so long
I wanted the past back, but now it's the future

that's burnished with possibility—the tang of saltwater,
diagonals of rain, vases of tulips looking out
a closed window on to snow. My grandfather
told me that a drowned man's shadow watches

from the water for him. As if death were a section
sheared off, just waiting for us to complete it. The bells
from the church on State Street don't break the day's
calm but seem to absolve it of all it contained,

errands & phone calls & pointless longing.
Maybe only in moments of transition are phantoms
visible: the one you are, the one I'll be. Then
I realize we're both phantoms, at least when paired,

& that there's a metabolism of the spirit as well
as of the body. Pagan religions were often territorial:
the wise traveler seeking out local gods as he entered
each new region. I'm moving through time, we all are,

& I wonder why there's no god whose office is bringing
dusk, someone I could revere by the simple act
of lighting candles or turning on lamps, & who might
be of help in the settling of my terrestrial accounts.

Counter Love

And now, *mon ange,* after nearly three years,
after breaking news that flashed, heaved its urgencies
at us, then disappeared, & what we called the death of God

was only the silence necessary for Him
to become meaningful again (too late for you,
too late for me), after all this & more I cannot name,

you have become text. A painting, a sonata, a nocturne:
you might have been one of Turner's lit storms,
a Rothko object where every plane rests

on a shadow of itself, or an annunciation
in which an intrusive element, disguised as light,
shifts the light. Schubert's C-major Quintet,

an Ellington indigo, Bill Monroe's high lonesome keening—
had I the chance I'd have chosen something other
than words. In the material world, legal heirs

& rightful eulogists, fists full of ashes I didn't scatter
in a city where I've never been. Ghosts coil in smoke;
left with the memory of a thousand conversations,

I scan the past for image-patterns, plot arcs, mood
concealed in setting: a dozen celadon bowls
where you placed spices for an elaborate soup;

the stone fence on Sixth Street, flakes of cierge & silver
erasing the statues in the garden as you touched
my hair, or was that later, in the weak yellow light

of the front hall. Who said what when. The index's
entries grow more connotative with each passing day,
the narrative less stable. After your death

I discovered lies that changed everything
& now know that what one is left with after finding
truth is not truth. Dark familiar, the orchestra's silent,

the room almost black. In the doorway,
the moon seeking something bright to shine on,
a rustle of nandina. And beyond, where I cannot see,

the thousand-leaved greens of the oaks.
A tenth season has turned, but neither
the past nor the future grows any smaller.

WHITE CENTER

A year is a reservoir, a basin, an indigo pool
where, fecklessly, I leave the lights on at night.
Otherwise water disappears into darkness
& I wake to the surface, pink & augural with dawn.
Rain lit by store windows, the wake of a speedboat,
the silvered charcoal of your remains—
a year is a reservoir holding these things.
The regulator's susurrus alerts me to the diver,
but he can't find you either. I'm standing in the shallows,
the kingdom of my grief twenty degrees hotter
than the water. A year is a room with aubergine walls;
it is a cupboard, a fruitwood cabinet, a drawer.
When a storm knocked out the power I lit candles
in front of the mirror, hoping to double the light,
but the breeze tossed them back & forth
until they disappeared into a single flame. On the ceiling
a bird, the shadow of a bird, or smoke.
In the cabinet I keep the glove of champagne kid
you pulled with your hand from mine,
a broken strand of coral beads, the Polaroid
of the UFO we spotted from the roof garden;
I keep the last fortnight we spent together
& all its weather, the fist of black tulle,

a citron strip of dawn. A year is a sack, a pocket,
a suitcase we carried through Britain one summer,
covered with stickers from India & Rome,
its silk lining gone iridescent where it frayed,
& it contains the view from our room of a meadow,
dazzling & lacustral. If I clipped
the seams & stretched the canvas of the bag
I might find the landscape you left unfinished,
a dogwood rinsing its final leaves in the lawn's
violet water. A year is a vessel, a glass,
a relucent vase of orchids & quatrains.
A packet of heirloom seeds, a large bowl holding
copper fish, the aura before migraine,
the secret glances mirrors exchange with mirrors
in an empty room, the acoustics of a bridge
& unseasonal snow. On the bridge a long cortege
over which a white heron rises. A year is a basket,
making ferric the skin of the ice it molds
or through which steam drifts & water sluices,
silver until it darkens dusk. Nothing can enclose you now.

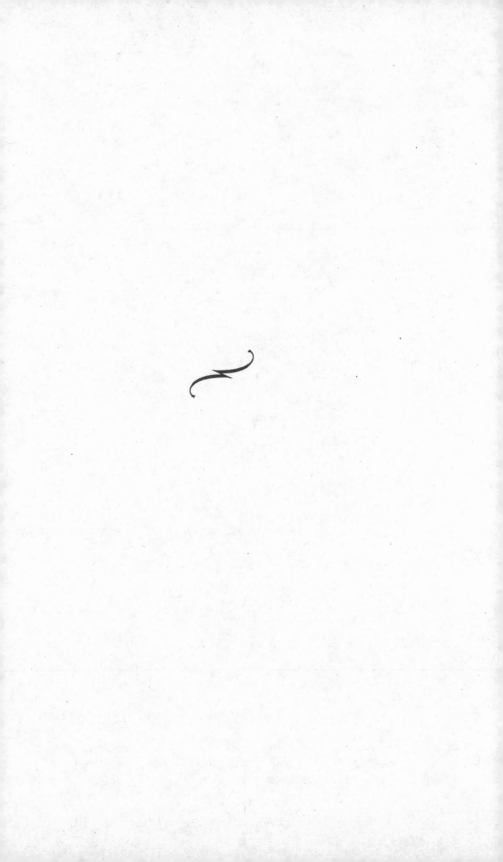

Acknowledgments

"White Center" appeared in *The Georgia Review*. "Song of the Abducted" and "The Yellow Point" appeared in *Hunger Mountain*. "In the Cathedral," *"Fin de Siècle,"* and "Spliced Solo" appeared in *The Louisville Review*. *"Tempo Rubato"* appeared in *North American Review*. "The Customary Mysteries, "Phantom Pain," and *"Brown, Black on Maroon"* appeared in *West Branch*. "Plaint" appeared in *In the Arms of Words: Poems for Disaster Relief*. "April Fifteenth" appeared in *River Styx* and was awarded second place in the 2005 *River Styx* International Poetry Contest.

The author is grateful to the Mississippi Arts Commission and the Greater Jackson Arts Council for grants that helped her complete this book.

Special thanks to Katie Blount and Betsy Bradley, Priscilla Barlow, Sarah Gorham, Jeffrey Skinner, James Patterson, Jon Salem, Austin Wilson, and everyone at JOA.

The Author

ALEDA SHIRLEY is the author of *Long Distance* (1996) and *Chinese Architecture* (1986), which won the Poetry Society of America's Norma Farber First Book Award. She has received fellowships from the National Endowment for the Arts, the Kentucky Arts Council, the Kentucky Foundation for Women, and the Mississippi Arts Commission. She lives in Jackson, Mississippi, with her husband, Michael McBride.